Passive Income Freedom

*Ideas & Strategies to Gain Multiple
Streams of Income by Investing in 2020*

Table of Contents

Introduction

We are currently living in one of the most dynamic times in history – THE TECHNOLGY ERA! For those who have tapped into the wealth of this season, the traditional 9-5 has become a thing of the past. People are making millions while sitting in the comfort of their own homes and travelling the world! To those who are not willing to take risks, this is simply too good to be true; but for those who are, this is the perfect time to get out of the rat race, abandon your J-O-B (just over broke) and make more money than you have ever dreamed of. The bottom line is that job security no longer exists, employees who thought they had a job for life are being made redundant in the thousands. The only job security you have today is to ensure that you are equipped with the right knowledge and skills to generate your own income.

The internet has opened the door to a number of opportunities that have enabled those with an entrepreneurial mindset to earn huge profits. However, may I remind you that as with all good things in life, you are going to have to put the work in, you are not going to become a millionaire overnight. This book is not a get rich quick gimmick, if that is what you are looking for, I apologize in advance, but I can't help you!

There are so many streams of passive income that it would be impossible for me to mention them all in this book. Therefore, I will focus on the most popular, you may be familiar with them or have heard about them in passing and want some more information, I intend on providing you with just that. I also want to do away with any misconceptions about passive income because there is a lot of false information out there, and the last thing you want is to invest in something that is not going to be profitable for you.

I advise that you take your time reading over each chapter, don't rush into anything too quickly and assess the pros and cons of every decision you intend on making.

I hope that the information provided in this book will launch you into the life of financial freedom that you deserve!

Chapter 1:

Understanding Passive Income

You may have heard about passive income, have a slight idea about it, or know nothing at all. In this chapter, I will be giving you an overview of exactly what passive income is so that you will have a better idea of what you are getting yourself into.

There are several definitions of passive income, but the most common is: *"Earning an income while you are not actively trying."* So, even if you are asleep, on vacation, or washing the dishes, you are earning money. Basically, its income being transferred into your bank account even though you are not directly working for it. One of the most common examples of passive income is rental income. You own the land that you rent to a horse rearer for $1000 per month. You will receive that money every month as long as the horse rearer is using the land.

Although you might think so, passive income is not a new phenomenon, it has been around since the beginning of time. However, it has significantly evolved over the years. Changes and advancements in the economy have provided us with an abundance of ways to generate passive income. For example, the ecommerce industry has opened the door for thousands of people to make money by selling products on Amazon and earning commission on sales.

The Importance of Passive Income

Passive income is essential if you want to achieve financial freedom, it is the smartest way to earn money. Think about this for a minute – there are only 24 hours in a day, you spend around eight of those hours asleep and even if you put in 16-hour work days, there is always going to be a cap on the amount of money you can make. Even if you are earning $10,000 an hour (which most people don't), you are still going to hit a glass ceiling in terms of your earning potential.

Not only does passive income enable you to generate cashflow in your sleep, you can earn an unlimited amount of money. Let's use Amazon as an example, just say you are selling a product for $20 a piece and 20,000 people per day are buying your product! Now, that's just one product, what if you were selling 50 products at the same rate?!

To some people, money isn't everything, they are happy to earn a little bit extra, but it is not a big priority in their life but spending time with family is. A passive income allows you to spend quality time with your family going to amusement parks, the movies, or on vacation without worrying about where the money is going to come from. You are no longer forced to work ridiculous hours to make ends meet. It is tough to get started, but once you are established, you are going to be making good money doing the bare minimum. That's the beauty of passive income, as time goes on it just gets easier as long as you are using the right strategies to scale your business. The work you do today, will continue to benefit you for months, and years down the line.

Chapter 2:

The Required Tools

Generating passive income is not for everyone; if you don't have the right mindset, you will fall flat on your face and you won't recover. Therefore, before you start, it is important to get into the right frame of mind.

Patience and determination are the most important attributes you are going to need to make this work. If this sounds like you, then you already have what you need to succeed. When it comes to generating passive income, the people who fail are those who give up too easily, things don't go their way and they get discouraged and throw in the towel. As I have already stated, this book isn't about getting rich quick, which is why if you don't have the determination you are going to find it extremely difficult to generate a passive income for yourself. It requires that you keep striving towards your goals for months before you start seeing results. For example, if you choose to start a blog and monetize it with affiliate products and advertisements, you are not going to start making an immediate income. It takes a lot of effort on your part to build a following, there is a possibility that you will either earn very little or nothing in the beginning. If you don't have patience and determination, you will give up very quickly.

Take Responsibility For the Outcome

Whether you succeed or fail, the responsibility is on you. Generating passive income is like any other journey in life, there are going to be ups and downs, you'll win some and you'll lose some. WHEN you fail, and I say WHEN because it will happen, don't start pointing fingers. Please understand that when it comes to success, failure is inevitable; there is not one successful person on the planet who walked into success without a struggle, it doesn't work like that. Neither is failure a bad thing; in fact, if you look at failure from the right angle, it will teach you a lot. You can use it as a springboard to launch you into the success that you desire. Finding the solution to a problem becomes easier when you accept that you are the one responsible for fixing it. Playing the blame game isn't going to get you any closer to the financial freedom you are looking for. There is no point in blaming the social media marketer you hired, or the freelance writer, or any other member of your staff because that isn't going to resolve the problem. The more time you spend pointing fingers, the less time you have to find a solution.

It is not uncommon for beginners to experience more failure than success; in saying that, the most seasoned entrepreneur fails. What matters is your response to failure, are you going to allow it to discourage you? Or are you going to use it to make smarter decisions when you try again. The most successful entrepreneurs take the latter approach.

Get a Mentor

The easiest way to become successful in a certain area is to work with a mentor – someone who has been where you are, understands the industry and knows what it takes to be successful. May I add that finding a mentor may be a challenge for you especially if you don't know anyone in the industry. However, there are plenty of people who are willing to help and will extend a helping hand to those who have a desire to succeed. Ask friends and family members, go through your social media contacts and contact people who you admire in the industry you are hoping to become a part of. It is also important to note that a mentor is going to challenge you, they are not just going to hand over the information to you on a plate, some people can get offended by this and quit because they feel as if they are wasting their time. Remember, there is no such thing as an easy life – whether you have a mentor or not, you are still going to have to work for what you want.

Adopt an Abundance Mindset

Your state of mind will determine your level of success, you must be able to see past your current circumstances in order to change them. So, you are not where you want to be in life, there is nothing wrong with that, what's important is that you know you have the power to change it. To every action there is an equal and opposite reaction, you reap what you sow. The same amount of energy you put into generating passive income is the same amount of energy you are going to get back. If your mind is focused on what's not going right, you will attract more of what's not working. I am in no way telling you to ignore the issues you are experiencing, you can't brush them under the carpet and expect them to go away. However, while you are finding solutions to the problems you are having, your main focus should be on achieving your goals. You must be determined to succeed and refuse to give up.

Failure to Plan Will Only Lead to Failure

Have you ever attempted to get to a destination that you were unfamiliar with without a GPS? The question sounds ridiculous because any rational person is going to ensure they have a GPS or precise directions before making their way. Why? Because you will end up getting lost and you will take a significantly longer time to get there than if you had planned your journey beforehand. Well, the same is true for generating a passive income, you must have a plan, or reaching your destination of financial freedom is going to be extremely difficult, if not impossible.

Outside of having the right mindset, goal setting and planning are two of the most important things you will need before you begin your journey to earning a passive income. You must identify both your short and long-term goals, as well as a time period for when you intend on achieving these goals. For example, once you have started, where can you see yourself in six months? Once you have determined your goals, you will then need to map out a plan to achieve those goals. You can call it the "blueprint" or the "masterplan." It also helps to break your goals down into small actionable steps so that you don't overwhelm yourself. The most important aspect of goal setting and planning is doing something every day to work towards your goals, even if it is something small, the aim is to ensure that your mind is constantly focused on your end goal!

Chapter 3:

Shopify

Ecommerce is one of the most lucrative businesses to invest in, and Shopify is one of the biggest players in online commerce. Thousands of merchants and entrepreneurs use the platform to sell their products with massive success. Shopify works well for two things, establishing a drop shipping business and starting an e-commerce store. There are several plans available to those who would like to use their services (these plans and rates as of October 2019 are as follows:

1. Basic Shopify: $29.00
2. Standard Shopify: $79.00
3. Advanced Shopify: $299.00
4. Shopify Plus: $2,000

One of the main advantages of Shopify is that they have a free trial version available for 14 days. This means that you can test out the platform to see if it works for you, if not, you can cancel your account without any financial penalty. If you decide to go ahead, choose one of the plans most suited to your budget and continue.

The platform is very simple to use, so those who are not tech friendly have nothing to worry about. Shopify has an inbuilt website builder and all you need to do is choose the template and customize it using the options and features they provide. Everything is self-explanatory and you are given step by step directions. You will also find that the templates have been designed for specific markets and niches, so the design is always going to be relevant to what you are selling.

If you are not selling your own products, not to worry, you can take the drop shipping route instead. So, instead of listing products that you will sell directly to the customer, you list products that you will order from suppliers or manufacturers once the customer makes their order. Drop shipping has grown in popularity over recent years because of how convenient the process is. You don't keep any inventory, and neither are you responsible for shipping the products to your customers. Once an order has been placed, your Shopify store orders the product from your supplier and they ship it to your customer. Your customers are not made aware of this process, as far as they are concerned, you are the one shipping them the products. The system is totally automated which means you are generating a lucrative passive income around the clock.

There are limited costs associated with selling products from a Shopify account, all you pay for is advertising, marketing and your Shopify plan.

Tips for Shopify Success

Start Slow

Don't jump in at the deep end, take advantage of the 14-day free trial to familiarize yourself with the features and functions.

Branding

Business such as Nike and Apple are so successful because of their brand. No matter what continent you are on, you are going to come across someone with these products. Therefore, it is important that you customize your online store so that it is unique and stands out from your competition. You should also bear in mind that there are going to be other people selling the same or similar products than you which makes it even more important that your brand is unique.

Focus on Quality

One of the mistakes that people make when they first start selling on Shopify is that they assume if they list a lot of products, they will achieve more sales. When it comes to building a business, this is not the best approach; your main focus should be quality and not quantity. Focus on ensuring that the one or two products that you do have meet the needs of your target audience and that they represent your brand.

Optimize Your Store

Your customers should be able to access your store from any device. Make sure your store is optimized so that it is accessible from laptops, desktops, cell phones and tablets.

User Friendly

A store that is not user friendly is going to send potential customers running straight into the arms of your competitors. We are living in an era where people no longer have the time to sit around trying to figure stuff out. If they find your website too difficult to navigate, they will click out within minutes and move onto the next. Remember, you are not the only person selling your product, it is very easy for your customers to look elsewhere.

Google Analytics

You need to know what's working with your store and what isn't, and Google analytics will give you access to exactly what you need to know. Shopify also has their own analytics program, but it is not as advanced as Googles.

Get Blogging

Shopify will provide you with a built-in blog, but you will need an additional blog to help direct traffic to your store. If you are not a fan of writing, hire a freelance writer (we will discuss more about this later on).

Free Giveaways

There are not many people who are going to turn down a freebie. Giving away free stuff will drive more customers to your site, increase engagement and ultimately generate more profit.

Email List

When it comes to sales, it is important to build solid regular customers that are always going to purchase your products. One way to achieve this is to build an email list of your existing clients so that you can send them regular updates about your store. People are only going to purchase your products if they know they are on sale.

Chapter 4:

Amazon Kindle

Pretty ironic considering Amazon Kindle is probably where you bought this book! And that's how I know for sure that you can make money here because I sell books on kindle all day long! Whether you think you can write or not, have the time to sit down and write a book or not, self-publishing is a really good way to generate a passive income.

One of the many advantages to publishing on Kindle is that there are no restrictions to what you can write about, fiction, non-fiction, short stories or novels – you name it, you can write about it. You can publish eBooks and paperbacks to ensure that you maximize your reach. You can set your own prices, and you own all the rights to the books you publish. If you decide that you want to add or remove a chapter in any of your books, you can do so at any time.

You can earn up to 70% in royalties and this applies to any country that has an Amazon market.

How to Write a Book

Decide what type of book you are going to write, it should be either fiction or non-fiction. According to my research, writers have had success in both areas; for fiction, romance novels do exceptionally well, and for non-fiction, how-to books are also a great hit. You can either write the book yourself or hire a ghostwriter from freelance websites such as www.upwork.com, www.peopleperhour.com or www.freelancer.com. It is important to mention that there are no set fees on these sites, freelancers charge according to their level of expertise, in most cases you will get what you pay for. No offense to anyone who is not a native English speaker, but when it comes to having a book written, it is advised that you hire a native English speaker to ensure that you get the best quality.

Cover Design

Strangely enough, the cover is the most important aspect of the book. Why? Because that is what potential customers see first; you could have a book written to best seller standards, and another book is just okay, but because the cover of the 'just okay' book is more appealing, guess what book people are going to buy? The 'just okay' book! So, unless you've got some graphic design skills hidden under your belt, it's advised that you hire a good graphic designer for your book cover. If you are really strapped for cash, you can use the Amazon in-house tools to generate a basic cover, no shade to Amazon, I wouldn't advise it if you really want your cover to pop. Again, you can hire a very good designer from a freelance website.

When it comes to graphic design, it doesn't matter whether the designer is a native English speaker or not, in fact I would suggest that you hire someone from the Philippines or India, they are very cheap and very talented. And by the way, it is not exploitation, since a fee of $30 is a lot to someone in a third-world country.

Get an Editor

Again, this is all down to your budget, but I would highly suggest that you hire an editor to ensure that your book doesn't contain any spelling mistakes or grammatical errors. Your readers will pick up on these things and won't feel in the least bit guilty about writing you a negative review. Afterall, they paid for a book, and they expect it to be written to a high standard. You might think that running your book through spell check or a site like Grammarly is enough, but most of the time it isn't. Again, unless you have some editing skills under your belt, it is best that you hire a professional editor from one of the freelance sites mentioned above.

Amazon Guidelines

Although they are not too strict, Amazon does have some guidelines that you need to follow. But don't worry, there is no need to read through them, when you publish your book, Amazon will let you know if you need to change anything.

Update Your Internet Browser

If you haven't done so already, make sure that your internet browser is updated, or you won't be able to access some of the features and functions within the Kindle publishing platform.

Sign up With KDP

If you already have an Amazon account, you can use it for the sign-up process. If not, you will need to create one – it only takes a couple of minutes, you just need to follow the instructions on the screen.

Once you are registered, go through the step by step process to publish your book. Amazon will send you a message stating that your book will be live within 48 hours. In my experience, it typically takes a couple of hours.

Once your book goes live, people will be able to purchase it all over the world.

During the set-up process, you will need to provide your bank account information for payment. Royalties are paid monthly, but they are paid 60 days after the month that they were earned. So, if you earned royalties in October, you will be paid at the end of December.

Tips for Success

Do Your Research

Some niches are more popular than others, but they are continuously changing, so before you start writing or hire someone to write, make sure that the niche you are writing about is going to generate a profit.

Free Chapters

Have you ever clicked on an Amazon book and attempted to click on it so you could get a preview of the book only to find that there wasn't one? How annoying was that! And how quickly did you click onto another book to find what you were looking for? Real quick right?! People want to get an idea of what they are buying, it's like going clothes shopping, there are very few people who walk into a clothes store, pick up what they like and pay for it. Most people try it on to find out whether it suits them or not. If it doesn't, they hang it up and keep looking for something that fits. The same is true when it comes to books, people want to read something they can relate to and if they don't like your writing style, they will keep clicking through books until they find something that suits them. Give your customers the opportunity to decide whether they want to purchase your book or not.

Get Your Book Reviewed

Before you do this, make sure your book is on point or you will find yourself disappointed because these people are not going to hold back from telling the truth. There are reviewers and bloggers in your niche who will happily read your book and review it. They will either write a spectacular review or speak about how much they enjoyed the book on their YouTube channel. However, it is important to mention that you shouldn't ask anyone to review your book in exchange for a free copy because this is against Amazon's policies and procedures. When you ask, you are simply asking for their honest opinion.

Start a Blog

If you really want to succeed as an author; write a blog. Your audience is going to want to know more about you and read other content you have written. This is a great way to build a following so that you have a solid group of buyers every time you release a new book.

Social Media

Whether it's via Facebook, Instagram, LinkedIn or all of them, make sure you have a social media presence. Its free and easy to use and you can use these platforms to engage with your audience.

Write a Series

When you write a series, readers wait in anticipation for the next book. Just think about authors such as Clive Cussler, Robert Ludlum and JK Rowling, they all made a name for themselves by writing book series. It's a clever strategy, and if it worked for them, it can work for you.

Collaborate With Other Writers

This is a powerful marketing strategy which enables you to glean off other authors target audience. Make sure that whoever you are collaborating with has a good reputation in the industry or you will find yourself in trouble.

Advertise Your Book

I am assuming you are reading this book because you want to make money, which means you are going to have to spend some money. The bottom line is that you may have written a bestseller, but if no one knows it exists, people are not going to buy it. A good place to start is Google AdSense, do your keyword research so that your ads will appear in the relevant blogs and websites related to the content of your book.

Giveaways and Contests

You can run these giveaways and contests on different platforms such as social media, your blog or your website. You can also use book promotion sites for advertisement purposes. Here are 127 of the top paid and free book promotion sites.

Myths About Kindle Publishing

You are going to hear a lot of stories floating around about what its like to publish a book on Kindle, and the majority of them are not true. You see, what happens is that you either get a lot of naysayers who tried it once and it didn't work for them, or people trying to generate a quick profit by selling lies.

- It's a Fast Way of Making Money: This is a BIG FAT LIE! The majority of self-published authors on Amazon make very little profit. The assumption is that you can just publish a book and Kindle will do all the work for you when the truth is that there are things you need to do in order to succeed and you should not expect to make any money by doing the bare minimum.

- You Must be Totally Unique: There is nothing new under the sun, everything has been done before so its literally impossible to be totally unique. You will find that people have similar titles and similar content to you, all this is irrelevant, as long as you are not copying someone else's content word for word, you will be fine.

- You Need to Have a Launch Party: Absolutely false! If you market your book properly and get it in front of the right audience, you won't need to have a launch party. You can if you want, but its an unnecessary expense when everything is so accessible online.

- There are too Many eBooks: This is true, there are plenty of eBooks, but as I said, as long as you market your book properly and get it in front of the right audience you will do well.

- You Need an Agent: Another lie! This is why it's called self-publishing, you can do it all on your own.

- Amazon Will Own Your Book: No, they won't; you own all the rights to your book, Amazon is just the platform that you are using to sell it which is why they take a small cut.

- You Need a Lot of Reviews to Appear High in Amazon's Search Results: Put this book down now and do me a favor. Hop over to Amazon and do a search on any title you are interested in. You will find that there are plenty of books that don't even have one review, but they are at the top of search results. Where your book will appear depends on several factors including keywords, book description, subtitle etc.

Chapter 5:

Fulfilment by Amazon

Amazon FBA (Fulfillment by Amazon) is one of the most profitable opportunities for entrepreneurs. No need to get your hands dirty on this one, as Amazon takes care of everything on your behalf – shipping, customer service, warehousing, the lot!

As you probably already know, Amazon is the largest online retailer in the world, so you don't need to build your own reputation, you are standing on the shoulders of a giant! There are plenty of people making millions selling products on Amazon and you can too if you follow the blueprint. Since Amazon does all the work, you can accomplish much more than you ever could on your own. You are able to scale a lot quicker and you can still run the business yourself even when you are selling millions of dollars' worth of products.

The Product Finding Process

Okay, so you want to start selling products on Amazon, the question is what do you sell? Not to worry, Amazon will give you the answer to this question and you won't need to buy some ridiculously high-priced software to do the searching for you. When it comes to finding products to sell, take a look at the products that are already selling well on the site. If you Google "Amazon best sellers," it will bring up all of the best-selling products on Amazon, you can check each department by clicking on it. As of October 2019, the best seller in toys and games is Monopoly, so now you know that everything on that list is making mad sales.

When checking out a market for a product, look at the review to revenue ratio, if a product has 1000 reviews and it has generated $100,000 in sales, it has a good ratio of $100 per review, but if there are 10,000 reviews and $100,000 in sales, that's $10 per review which isn't good news. This is the fastest and easiest way to determine whether the market is already saturated and where a product is in its lifecycle.

A good site to use for sales analytics is www.junglescout.com, it provides you with a breakdown of the competition for every search. Once you have typed in your request, the site provides you with a full page of data. From daily sales costs to revenue, everything you will need to identify whether a market is worth investing in is on this site.

The smartest thing to do when it comes to finding products to sell on Amazon is to stay niche. It makes no sense to compete with 1000 other sellers for the same product. When you are doing your research, put your buyers hat on; when a customer types in "electric kitchen utensils," it is clear they are just browsing, but when they get a bit more specific and type in "electric tin opener," for whatever reason, they need that tin opener and they are looking to make a purchase. Your focus should be on products that people need and not want, people are more likely to buy necessities before they buy wants.

If you are going to take your chances in the ecommerce space, you will need to be creative and find unique marketing methods for your niches, you should also focus on finding niches that are yet to be developed. A very smart idea is to look for a niche within a niche. Stay away from products that are in high demand, things with a lot of moving parts and electronics.

Pay Attention

According to the experts, the easiest part of the process is finding the right products to sell, but the people who are trying to get their foot in the door say it's the hardest. They are afraid to choose a product that's got too much competition, and neither do they want to pick a product that's not going to sell. Don't become one of these people! They never get started!

Retailers

The next time you go to a store such as Wal-Mart or Target, pay attention to the products on the shelves, especially the ones that are at eye level. They are placed there for a reason – so you can see them, because they are the most profitable products. The store owners want you to buy those products because they generate the most profit, and they could also generate the most profit for you.

Informercials

Some of those annoying infomercials could actually turn out to be a goldmine for you. Whoever is selling these products are making some serious money or they wouldn't waste their time, there is a demand for those products which means that there is also going to be a demand for them on Amazon.

I Know What Products to Sell – Now What?

The majority of private label products you see on Amazon come from the supplier www.alibaba.com. It's pretty simple to find a good supplier because they are independently assessed on certain criteria and the good ones will have a gold star rating. You also have access to how long each company has been in business so that you know they are not scam artists. If you are looking for hand towels because they came up on the best sellers list during your research, type in "hand towels" on the Alibaba site and it will present you with a list of suppliers.

How do I Know I am Going to Make a Profit?

Good question…..after all, that's why you're here isn't it? Ok so once you conducted your Google search you have found that yoga mats are a bestselling product on Amazon. You then go to Alibaba and find that it typically costs between $5-7 per yoga mat. You don't want to make the mistake of selling products that are too cheap, so the general rule of thumb is to price them between $15 -$50. This is a good price range because consumers are not going to need to think too much about spending that amount of money unless they are completely broke! So basically, things are more likely to sell at that price. If you price your yoga mat at $25, and the shipping costs are $4.50 per unit, and you pay $7.50 Amazon fees (30%), you

are going to make a $13 profit on each unit sold –
that's more than 50% profit!

Private Labelling

Private labelling is when you put a name on a
generic product so that you can sell it for more
money. You might be selling a no-name watch for
$50 but put a name on it and you will be able to sell
it for $75. You will need to come up with private
label packaging and branding but it's not hard, just
pick a name that people will remember, buy a
domain and have a website built with a custom
email so it all looks professional. You can go to one
of the freelance websites like www.upwork.com,
www.peopleperhour.com, or www.fiverr.com
and have a designer create a logo and a website.
This is the fastest way to legitimize your product,
do it now or risk loosing out on huge profits.

Selling Your Product

Now that you've figured out what products to sell and you are ready to go, the next step is to create your listing. Remember, whatever product you are selling, it's a niche product that people need; when it comes to the product keywords, you must be very specific so that whatever you are listing shows up in the top results when potential customers do a search. A great way to do this is to take a look at your competitors negative reviews and turn them around when making your listing. How are you going to fix the issues that customers are having with your competitors' products? Let's just say you are selling notice boards, and one of the main complaints is that they are too heavy, so they keep falling off the walls. Make sure that you mention in your description that the boards are "light enough to hang on the wall without falling off." This way when a customer is scrolling through the reviews of your competitor and that is something that bothers them, they are more likely to buy from you instead.

Pictures For Your Listing

You will need a lot of high-quality pictures for your listing as people are more interested in what they see than what they read. The joke is that a lot of Amazon sellers don't even get this part right, but they still make plenty of money. Just take a look at the average picture on Amazon – they are not the best! Show how your products are used in everyday life, if they can be used in different situations, show that too.

Product Benefits

Forget the features! Consumers are not interested in the features of a product, they want to know what it can do for them, at the end of the day they are buying it for a reason. So instead of talking about the thickness of your yoga mats (a feature) say that the mat is thick enough to protect your hands and knees and provide additional comfort while performing exercises (benefit).

Reviews

Remember, think like a buyer? Have you ever purchased a product that didn't have any reviews? You have probably answered no to this question and the reason is that you want some sort of evidence that you can trust the product. If the majority of the reviews are negative, you are not going to buy the product. You can start by asking friends and family members to buy your product and review it.

Advertising

Once you have got some reviews under your belt, start using Amazon ads to drive more traffic to your products. When you are on the Amazon site

and you see a product with the word "sponsored"
attached to it, that's an Amazon ad. It is going to
cost you some money, but remember, you need to
spend money to make money.

Just do it!

I don't care how broke you are, I know you can
find $50 somewhere to get this started, most
people get stuck in a J-O-B because they are too
scared to start anything else, they want to know
the answer to every question before they put their
foot on the gas. LISTEN! You will never make
money if you are not willing to take any risks!

Chapter 6:

Real Estate

Research states that 90% of millionaires in the world made the majority of their fortune by investing in real estate! However, if you don't have much money to spare then real estate probably isn't for you, (please don't fall for those no money down scams, you will end up in trouble), but if you can raise the cash, go for it! Before I go any further, I would like to recommend a fantastic real estate forum, it's where I got the majority of my information from, check it out here: www.biggerpockets.com. It's a community of both seasoned investors and newbies who are interested in real estate. You will find a lot of good advice on this site.

BRRRR (No it's not a typo)

BRRRR is the acronym for Buy Rehab Rent Refinance Repeat, I swiped this strategy off the biggerpockets website. It involves purchasing a property that needs a bit of work, fixing it up, renting it out, refinancing to get some cash and then repeating the process until you have built the property portfolio that you desire. There are plenty of people on this site who now earn more than 25 properties because of this strategy. It allows you to keep buying properties without ever running out of money to invest. Let's delve deeper into each step of the BRRRR process.

Buy

To start, if you are going to invest in real estate, you need a property; but this doesn't mean that you should go out and blow your cash on the first house you find, you need to spend some time searching for the best deal. The strategy basically involves flipping houses, but instead of selling the house once you have completed the renovations, you rent it out. As long as you got a good deal, the rental income will provide you with monthly cash flow.

The general rule of thumb when it comes to real estate flipping is the 70% rule, and it states that you should never pay more than 70% of a properties after repair value (ARV), minus the cost of the repairs. This is the amount the property will be worth after completing the renovations.

If you are going to be successful in the real estate business, it's going to take some work. You can't just expect the deals to fall into your lap. You will need to keep sending out emails, checking different websites and driving around town to find the best deals.

The catch is that when it comes to making your first purchase, you are not going to find a traditional lender willing to give you a loan on a property that needs renovating. This means that you will need to find another way to find the money, whether it's taking equity out of the home you now own, dipping into savings etc.

Rehab

Rehab is the second part of the BRRRR strategy, and it involves renovating the property you have just acquired. As mentioned, you won't be flipping the property once the repairs have been completed, you will be renting it out to tenants. This means you will need to choose materials that are going to provide you with the highest rental price, it is also important that these materials are durable. What you don't want is to use bad quality materials that you will need to replace every couple of years. During the rehab process, you must remember that your aim is to get the highest ARV and rent per month. So, if you find a two-bedroom property that is big enough to add a third bedroom, then that is what you do. Not only will this increase the value of the home and provide you with more equity, it will also add additional cash to your monthly cash flow.

It is also important to mention that you should never attempt to cut corners when renovating. Some people will do this to save money, but it backfires later on down the line when your tenants are calling you every other day because something isn't working in the house. Therefore, make the initial investment so that you avoid issues like this in future. I am in no way saying you should ignore your budget when it comes to rehab, but if you do things the right way, you can still cut costs.

Rent

Rent is the most important part of this strategy when looking at it from a passive income perspective. The aim here is to make sure you rent the property out to good tenants, obviously you want people who are going to be able to afford the rent, but you also want high-class responsible tenants who are not going to trash the place. This is why location is important; granted, you are going to get cheaper properties in a run-down part of town, but that also means you will have a higher chance of getting low-class tenants. It is advised that you have all tenants complete a rental application that involves a credit and a background check. Negative information like bad credit or missed rental payments should act as a red flag not to rent to them.

Refinance

The next step is to refinance the property into a conventional comfortable mortgage. But wait................didn't you just say a few pages back that it's more or less impossible to get a traditional lender to give you a mortgage on a property that needs renovating? Yep, that's what I said; however, once the place has been renovated, that's a whole different story! After a house has been flipped, the interest rates are lower, they are a long-term stable investment and they are typically extremely easy to get.

There is also the possibility that you won't need to finance your property to get your money back. Maybe you have enough money that you can afford to leave your initial investment in the property. This may even help you get a better monthly cash flow and return on your investment. However, it can be just as beneficial to refinance and get your money back so that you can repeat the process.

Using the same example I used earlier, let's say you purchased a property that has an ARV of $100,000 and bought it for $55,000, you spend $15,000 on renovations which means you have invested a total of $15,000 into the property. The majority of lenders will allow you to refinance a property for 70% of the ARV, which means that you have the chance of getting your $70,000 back. Once you have refinanced the property and rented it out, you will own a house that not only generates passive income but also holds around 30% in equity!

Repeat

The final part of the strategy is to repeat, this is where you will start really making some money. You are repeating because it worked the first time so there is no reason why it shouldn't work the second, third and fourth time. However, you can only take out 10 mortgages, but that's great news if you have 30% equity in each property and you only spent your original investment and made it back on each property!

Chapter 7:

Blogging

Blogging has become a very popular way of generating online passive income. However, it takes a lot of hard work and a long time before you start making any money from blogging. But once you have everything up and running, it will become a goldmine that requires very little input on your end.

If your blog is going to be successful, it is important that you provide valuable content to your visitors? What does it mean to create value? Your content should be able to help your readers in some way. Find a niche that you are passionate about so that you don't get bored and give up. You don't want to blend in, your aim should be to stand out from the crowd like a big neon light.

If you check out most blogs in the same niche, you will find that they all provide the same information, reworded and with different titles. This is where you can gain a competitive advantage, by providing content that is completely unique. Think like a reader, if you were searching for information on a particular subject, what would you want to read? How would you like your visitors to speak about your blog when they are having conversations with their friends? You want them to be excited and enthusiastic and speak about it as if they have just found something absolutely magnificent. Maybe your blog is about different beauty techniques and you can show your readers how to transform themselves into bombshells. Whatever your blog is about, just make sure it is helping people solve their problems.

How to Start a Blog

The first step is to buy a domain name and set up your hosting services, you can use platforms such as HostGator, BlueHost, and GoDaddy for this. Once you have signed up, fill out all the information and choose a plan, a good place to start is the one-year plan.

WordPress Installation

The next step is to log into your hosting provider account and select the option to install WordPress. For now, everything should be left at their default settings, it is advised that you deselect the plugins box and recommended themes, we will go into this later. Select complete and you will have successfully installed WordPress. Make sure that you write down your login details and password information.

After you have logged into your site, you are given access to your WordPress screen, it's simple to use, so even if you are not the techy type, you won't have any problems.

The first step will be to change the name of your site so that it works with your domain. If your blog is about beauty techniques, the name should be beauty related. Select: "Settings> General, you will see "Site Title," enter your site name in this field, your tagline should also be updated at this point, once the site is live, you will find it under your title. After all the changes have been made, click on "Save" at the bottom of the screen.

Permalinks

A permalink is the URL of the content that is published to your WordPress site, when someone wants to view one of your pages, the permalink is what they enter into their address browser; and search engines and other sites use them to link to your website. This means that permalinks are very important when it comes to your sites searchability.

You will find your permalinks by going to Settings> Permalinks, it is all pre-populated, but you will still need to make a few changes. Select "Custom Structure" and copy and paste this: /%category%/%postname%/

Choosing a Theme

There are thousands of themes for you to choose from on WordPress, some are free, others are paid. Select "Appearance" > "Themes" > "Wordpress.org Themes" and all the themes you could possibly imagine will come up. Once you have found one that you like, select "Install" and then "Activate." After the site has been activated, you can then go on to write your first post.

How to Publish a Post

You don't need to be a rocket scientist to publish a post on WordPress, everything is very self-explanatory. Just go to "Posts" and select "Add New," a box will come up saying "Enter title here," you then enter the title of your post and then type the content. Once you have written and edited it, hit "Publish," a message will come up on the screen saying, "Post Published," and that's it, your first post has been published!

Contact Me

If any of your visitors want to contact you, they can do so through a contact form, but you will need to set this up yourself. Go to "Pages" > "Add New," type "Contact Me" in the title box and type a short message to your visitors, you can say something like: "If you have any comments or questions about this post, send me a message and I will get back to you as soon as I can."

Your page is now fully functioning! Before making your site public, you are shown a "Coming Soon" page when you log onto the site. It is shown to you on every page in the WordPress builder. Select "Click here" and you will see a message saying "Congratulations!" You are then shown another "click here" button, click on that and it will allow you to view your blog as your viewers see it.

You can now customize the site by changing colors, adding photos and making it your own.

Create a Brand

Have you ever wondered why names like Nike, Adidas and Apple are so popular? It's because of branding! I don't know what is more famous, the logo or the name, but you can start by having a logo designed because this is how people will remember you when you post something. Your logo is what will distinguish you from your competitors. Don't get any old logo, make sure its spectacular so that people will remember your brand.

How to Monetize Your Blog

If you are reading this book you are not starting a blog for fun, you are doing it so you can generate passive income. When it comes to monetization, it is not something you can do straight away, you need to grow your following by providing consistent rock-solid content. I can't tell you when the right time is to start monetizing your site, some people start in a couple of months, others take years. It's up to you to decide. So here are some of the most effective and common monetization strategies to get you started:

Sell Information Products

By this point, your visitors know that your content is nothing but the best, they trust you to give them exactly what they need when they need it. Now you can start charging for some of this content, you may feel a bit uncomfortable doing this since you have been giving it away for free for so long, but trust me, people are willing to pay for what they need especially when they know they can't get it anywhere else. You can also create a training course or an eBook and post it on your site for sale, for additional revenue, you can also post them on sites like Udemy, Amazon and Clickbank. However, you will have already built trust with your followers so this is where the majority of your sales will come from.

Make it a Membership Site

Your blog is where your visitors come to get valuable information; however, if they want even more valuable content than what they are already getting, they will have to pay for it. This is where you set up a members only page where paid subscribers have access to premium content. You should have established yourself as an authority in your niche by now so it shouldn't be difficult to convert the visitors you already have into paying subscribers, even if you can't convert all of them, you will be able to convert a high percentage; Afterall, where else are they going to go to get such high quality content?

Personal Consulting and Coaching

This isn't a passive income strategy, but you can make some very good money by taking this route. If you really know your stuff, and you can prove your success in that area, people are going to pay for one on one coaching or consulting with you. There are some gurus who charge $25,000 for their services and people are paying without even thinking twice.

Sell Physical Products

In most cases, whether you can get away with selling physical products on your blog will be determined by your niche; but if you can, go for it.

You have been solving problems on behalf of your subscribers for some time now, but instead of solving the problem for them directly, you can create a software that will solve it for them. Subscribers will need to pay a monthly fee for access to the software.

Affiliates

When it comes to making money through affiliates, only advertise products that relate to your specific niche and that you have used yourself. It would make no sense trying to sell dog grooming products when your blog is about golf! With affiliates, you post a link to the product on your site, and each time a sale is made, you get a cut.

Sell Your Site

Once you have done all the hard work and made some good money from your blog, sell it. There are people who make a very good living from buying blogs, redesigning them and selling them. If your site is profitable enough, you can get thousands of dollars for it.

Chapter 8:

Authority Sites

An authority website is one that gains the trust of its readers because of its high-quality content, and the amazing experience that it delivers. To build an authority website, you must give people a reason to come to your site by solving their problems.

How to Build an Authority Website

When it comes to building a top-notch authority site, there are several things you will need to take into consideration, these include the following:

- The website is focused on one specific niche.
- The websites solve problems for visitors.
- The main focus of the website is not about promoting affiliates so that the owner can make money.

- The website is focused on building the trust of the reader, engaging with them and focuses on user interaction.

- The owner of the website engages with users on social media and the comments section.

If you are an expert in any field, creating an authority site can be very profitable. Over time, authority sites can quite easily make a six-figure income if it is delivering superior content for its users. Jon Gillham is the owner of www.authoritywebsiteincome.com and several other online businesses. His websites became so profitable for him that he was able to quit his day job as an engineer and consistently makes between $10,000 and $16,000 a month from his websites. He states that an authority site is one that adds value and doesn't just rehash information that people can google, it's a site that provides unique content that solves problems for the user.

When you have experts writing the content for you, its much easier to create an authority site because they know what they are talking about and will have access to research materials that the average person doesn't have. A good example of an authority site is one which provides a tool to solve the problem that is being talked about such as a downloadable program or an online calculator.

Identifying a Market

You will find your authority site market in the same way you will for your Amazon products, eBooks etc.; by finding a niche. You want to choose a broad, solid market, so let's say you decide to go for golf, you then choose a sub-niche within the golf market such as disabled golfers, and that will be the main topic for your website. It is extremely important that your sub-niche market has items to sell, because when it comes to monetizing your site, affiliate marketing will be one of your main money makers.

You will then need to focus on keyword research, your sub-niche should have some low-competition keywords to drive traffic to your site. You can use Google AdWords to look up keywords. You should look at keywords from a market standpoint, so don't find a keyword and base your site around that; instead, find a specific problem that your website is going to help people solve and then find the keywords related to that problem. You will need to look for a certain set of metrics within those keywords which are high volume and low competition. You can use a keyword research tool at www.longtailkeywordpro.com for your keyword research.

How to Create Superior Content

Google is not the same as it used to be, when this online game first started, people could rank on Google using a strategy called keyword stuffing and the quality of the content was not the main focus. However, things have drastically changed, and today, the best content is rewarded with higher rankings. Once you have great content, everything else will fall into place. So, start by deciding that you are going to create the best content in your niche, and build on that. If you are an expert in your topic, then its not going to be difficult to come up with superior content; however, if you are not an expert, you may need to find someone else that is to produce your content. You can do this by outsourcing content to freelancers on sites such as www.upwork.com, www.peopleperhour.com, or www.freelancer.com.

How to Monetize Your Site

There are plenty of ways in which you can monetize your authority website; here are some of them:

Direct Leads

In this scenario, there is an insurance broker who is on the lookout for new customers. Your site is focused on helping first time fathers understand insurance; you create a page that states: "Here is everything you need to ask your insurance broker to ensure that your family is protected as a new dad, click on this link so that someone from the industry can contact you and provide you with more valuable information." Now you have a list of a ton of first-time fathers who have signed up for that site, you can then sell that list to insurance brokers who will pay you plenty of money to have access to such a targeted list of potential clients.

Affiliates

When you first get started with your authority site, it should be completely free and focused on providing your visitors with plenty of helpful information to assist them in solving the problems they have. The next logical step is for them to purchase whatever they need to fix that problem. For example, if your site is about mortgages, and a reader is looking for information on where they can get a mortgage, you provide them with the options through your site and then get paid a commission if the individual takes out a mortgage through one of those options you provided.

Chapter 9:

Digital Real Estate

Digital real estate? Now what on earth is that? It's basically investing in websites – sound too good to be true? There is a huge market for it – let me tell you all about it. There are three main ways you can make money with websites:

1. Developing websites
2. Flipping websites
3. Domain name parking

Developing Websites

With this method, you buy a domain name, have a website built, develop the site and then start generating a profit from the site. You will make the most profit out of developing websites, but it is a slow process and it will take some time before you start to generate a profit.

Flipping Websites

In the same way you can flip houses, you can flip websites; website flipping involves purchasing a website, developing a website and then selling it for a profit.

How to Flip a Website

Let's take it back to the real estate analogy, you find a property that's in pretty bad shape, its selling for cheap so you buy it, you increase its value by fixing it up and then put the property back on the market and make a profit. When it comes to website flipping, you can either buy a brand-new domain name and develop the website, or you can purchase a website that has already been developed, fix it up, raise the value and then sell it.

It is also important to mention that if you don't know anything about websites, you will probably need to hire an expert to take care of the development phase for you. You will find plenty of freelance web developers on the following sites: www.upwork.com, www.peopleperhour.com, or www.freelancer.com.

Domain Name Parking

This is the easiest and cheapest form of website investing; for your initial investment, all that is required is the cost of the domain name which is typically a few dollars. Once you have purchased that domain name, you own it and no one else can use it. If you have thought of an awesome domain name, buy it now before someone else thinks of it. The website will then display a "Under Construction," or "Coming Soon" message to its visitors. You can leave the domain name like this for as long as you want, registration for a year, but you can renew it once it reaches the expiry date.

If you want to start developing the website, you will need to buy hosting, once it is hosted, the website is no longer a parked website. This all sounds great, but how do you make money from parking a domain name? Absolutely NOTHING! All you need to do is hold onto it until someone comes along and desperately wants to use your awesome website name, but they can't because you own it. The ball is now in your court as to how much you want to sell it for. If the person is desperate enough, they will pay.

When it comes to choosing a website name, the key is to focus on niche topics and keywords that a business will want.

Think about domain name parking in terms of physical real estate; so just imagine there's a large piece of land up for sale in the middle of a rural area and its really cheap because nothing has been built on it. However, there is a fancy shopping mall up the road which is just about to open for business. This is an indication that the land is going to be worth a lot more in a few years' time once the area begins to develop and there is a spike in demand. So, when the location becomes a bustling commercial center, people are going to have no problems paying a much higher price for it than your original investment. Now you can make a large profit because when you bought it, you were thinking about what people will want in the future. You saw the potential in that derelict piece of land.

The same principle applies to domain name parking; your initial investment is going to be cheap because the domain isn't worth anything right now. However, if you choose a good name, it will be worth a lot to someone in the future.

Selling Your Website

Whether you are selling a developed website or a domain name, you can do so on one of the following sites:

www.flippa.com

Flippa.com is currently the most popular and largest arena to buy and sell websites. You can even buy apps and domains, with more than 700,000 buyers and sellers on the site, you are almost guaranteed to find a buyer for your niche.

www.empireflippers.com

If you don't want to deal with the hassle of selling your website yourself, this site will take care of everything on your behalf, and they have built a reputation for being the best in the business. Here are some tips to get your website sold for the highest price:

Attention to Detail: While most buyers are not going to be too bothered about the odd spelling mistake, a site that is riddled in mistakes isn't going to do very well. Therefore, have an editor go over the content before putting your website up for sale.

Be Descriptive: When it comes to writing a description for your website, think like a buyer, what information would you like to have access to? Would you buy a website that barely came with any details? You will assume the owner had something to hide, when it comes to auctions on these selling sites, the websites that don't sell are the ones that don't have a good description. At the top of the auction copy, you should have a high-level overview or summary of the website, the remainder of the description should be used to dig into specific details. Break up the text with headers so that your readers have easy access to the information they want.

Transparency: When it comes to sales, people prefer to buy from people they trust, like and know. While building rapport is impossible when selling at an auction, you might want to think about reaching out to potential buyers through your social media profiles, so put a link to your blog, Facebook page etc. on your auction copy. In this way people can contact you if they wish and you are showing that you are a real person with nothing to hide. Since the majority of sellers prefer to remain anonymous, you can gain a competitive advantage by being transparent.

Don't Oversell: Most buyers are very skeptical about statements such as: "This $1000 site can easily generate $2000 in a couple of weeks." If this was true, why are you selling it? There is nothing wrong with being positive about the potential of your site; however, just make sure you are being truthful. One way you can avoid overselling or even underselling for that matter is not to focus on figures when describing the sites potential. The truth of the matter is that you won't be able to accurately predict how much your site could generate in the future. Whoever buys it will do so because they see potential, the money they make will depend on what they choose to do with the site.

Build Trust and History: If selling sites is something you want to do often, you will need to build a solid reputation and trust within this space. All auctions have a watchers or viewers feature where sellers are watched by buyers. www.flippa.com also has a "Watched Seller" feature where emails are sent out to watchers when a seller they follow has listed a new website for sale. To build trust, it is also a good idea to undersell but overdeliver, in this way, buyers are impressed, and you will reap plenty of positive reviews.

Keep Your Eye on Savvy Buyers: Savvy buyers attempt to lock the auction by putting in their best bid early to deter anyone else from bidding. Don't fall for this strategy and wait it out, there is a possibility that someone else may put in a higher bid.

Promote Outside of the Website: Whatever website you are selling on don't rely on them for sales. Promote outside of the website using your social media profiles, discussion boards and blog posts to drive traffic to your auction.

Conclusion

NOW GET ON WITH IT! Don't become one of those people who read every book, attend every seminar and take every course but never get started. There is a reason why only 1-2% of the population earn the majority of the world's wealth. No, it's not because they have more opportunities than the average person, no its not because of where they were raised or because of the families they were born into – it's because they saw an opportunity and they took it. They worked extremely hard and made it work for them.

It's time to stop dreaming, stop complaining about what you don't have but wish you had and start doing. Remember, persistence and determination is the name of the game. If you are going to give up at the first hurdle you encounter, you are not cut out for success, stick to your 9-5 and continue making someone else rich, retire at 65, move to Florida and live in your little retirement home! This might sound harsh, but some of you need to hear it!

Rise and shine people, there is enough money in the world for everyone to have Bill Gates money ten times over, which is why I wrote this book. I want you to experience the same financial freedom that I am enjoying and will continue to enjoy for the rest of my days!

There are plenty of ideas in this book for you to choose from, don't skim through the chapters, if you have, go back and read it again. Find a strategy that resonates with you and get to work!

I wish you every success on your passive income journey!